DENMARK

Big Buddy Books
An Imprint of Abdo Publishing
abdopublishing.com

Julie Murray

abdopublishing.com

Published by Abdo Publishing, a division of ABDO, PO Box 398166, Minneapolis, Minnesota 55439.
Copyright © 2018 by Abdo Consulting Group, Inc. International copyrights reserved in all countries. No part of this book may be reproduced in any form without written permission from the publisher. Big Buddy Books™ is a trademark and logo of Abdo Publishing.

Printed in the United States of America, North Mankato, Minnesota.
052017
092017

THIS BOOK CONTAINS
RECYCLED MATERIALS

Cover Photo: Shutterstock.com.
Interior Photos: Frank Bach/Alamy Stock Photo (p. 25); Roberto Cornacchia/Alamy Stock Photo (p. 21); De Luan/Alamy Stock Photo (p. 16); Francis Joseph Dean/Deanpictures/Alamy Stock Photo (p. 19); epa european pressphoto agency b.v./Alamy Stock Photo (pp. 27, 29); INTERFOTO/Alamy Stock Photo (p. 17); ©iStockphoto.com (pp. 13, 34); Dennis Jacobsen/Alamy Stock Photo (p. 38); John Peter Photography/Alamy Stock Photo (p. 35); Lebrecht Music and Arts Photo Library/Alamy Stock Photo (p. 31); Naturfoto-Online/Alamy Stock Photo (p. 35); Sean Pavone/Alamy Stock Photo (p. 5); Kim Petersen/Alamy Stock Photo (p. 13); Patrycja Polechonska/Alamy Stock Photo (p. 15); Niels Poulsen/Alamy Stock Photo (p. 23); Niels Quist/Alamy Stock Photo (p. 9); jon ryan/Alamy Stock Photo (p. 11); Shutterstock.com (pp. 23, 34, 37); Rick Strange/Alamy Stock Photo (p. 11); Stringer – Imaginechina (p. 33); Jochen Tack/Alamy Stock Photo (p. 31); Grethe Ulgjell/Alamy Stock Photo (p. 35); Zoonar GmbH/Alamy Stock Photo (p. 19).

Coordinating Series Editor: Tamara L. Britton
Editor: Katie Lajiness
Graphic Design: Taylor Higgins, Keely McKernan

Country population and area figures taken from the CIA World Factbook.

Publisher's Cataloging-in-Publication Data

Names: Murray, Julie, 1969- , author.
Title: Denmark / by Julie Murray.
Description: Minneapolis, MN : Abdo Publishing, 2018. | Series: Explore the countries | Includes bibliographical references and index.
Identifiers: LCCN 2016962348 | ISBN 9781532110481 (lib. bdg.) | ISBN 9781680788334 (ebook)
Subjects: LCSH: Denmark--Juvenile literature.
Classification: DDC 948.9--dc23
LC record available at http://lccn.loc.gov/2016962348

DENMARK

CONTENTS

AROUND THE WORLD

Our world has many countries. Each country has beautiful land. It has its own rich history. And, the people have their own languages and ways of life.

Denmark is a country in Europe. What do you know about Denmark? Let's learn more about this place and its story!

Did You Know?

Danish is Denmark's official language.

Tivoli Gardens features shops, restaurants, and shows. It is near Copenhagen City Hall.

PASSPORT TO DENMARK

Denmark is in western Europe. Most of the country is on a **peninsula** called Jutland. The North Sea and the Baltic Sea surround Denmark. Germany is to the south. Nearby islands and Greenland belong to Denmark.

Denmark's total area is 16,639 square miles (43,094 sq km). More than 5.5 million people live there.

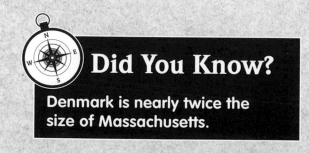

Did You Know?

Denmark is nearly twice the size of Massachusetts.

WHERE IN THE WORLD?

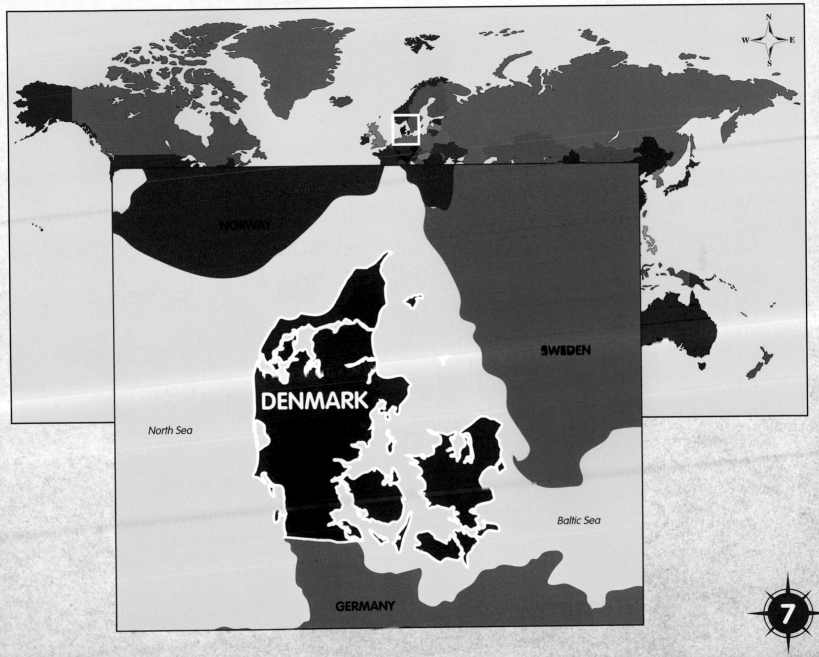

NORWAY

SWEDEN

DENMARK

North Sea

Baltic Sea

GERMANY

IMPORTANT CITIES

Since 1443, Copenhagen has been Denmark's **capital**. More than 1.2 million people live there. In the mid-1000s, Copenhagen began as a fishing village. Its harbor allowed for trading with far-off countries. Today, Copenhagen is home to Denmark's major port.

In the city, many people travel on bicycles. Copenhagen has special lanes and bridges for bikes. Local buses and trains are also popular ways to get around.

SAY IT

Copenhagen
koh-puhn-HAY-guhn

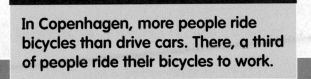

In Copenhagen, more people ride bicycles than drive cars. There, a third of people ride their bicycles to work.

DENMARK

Copenhagen

Århus is Denmark's second-largest city, with almost 260,000 people. In the 1800s, the city grew its railroads and harbor. Today, Århus continues to have a busy port and a large **economy**. Major businesses produce chemicals, clothes, iron, and timber.

Odense is the third-largest city. About 172,000 people live there. The city was established around the year 1000. In 1247, much of Odense burned down. The city was rebuilt and today, local factories make **electronics** and machines.

The Cathedral of St. Clemens was built in the 1100s. Located in the center of Århus, it has the highest steeple in Denmark.

SAY IT

Århus
AWR-hoos

Odense
OH duhn-suh

Built in 1554, Egeskov Castle is in Odense. It stands in the middle of a lake. The water helped protect the castle from attacks.

Denmark in History

Denmark has a long history. From the 800s to the 1000s, the **Vikings** took over much of Europe. Denmark eventually ruled parts of England, Germany, Norway, and Sweden.

In 1397, Queen Margaret united Denmark, Norway, and Sweden in the Union of Kalmar. A king and queen ruled until 1523. During the 1600s and 1700s, Denmark fought to control multiple countries.

After hundreds of years of fighting, the Danes wanted peace. They worked toward peaceful relations with other countries. And in 1915, new laws gave the Danes more rights.

The Jelling Orm is a model Viking ship. Today, it is one of few freshwater Viking ships.

Frederick VII ruled Denmark from 1848 to 1863. His statue is in Copenhagen.

The country did not choose sides during both **World War I** and **World War II**. However, Germany still took over its government in 1940.

In 1973, Denmark became a member state in the **European Union** (EU). The country joined at the same time as Ireland and the United Kingdom.

Since the 1990s, the Danes have struggled with **immigration**. And, they remain undecided on their relationship with the rest of Europe. They are one of few EU countries to not use the euro as currency.

Christiansborg Palace is a government building in Copenhagen. After a fire in 1907, the palace was rebuilt for the third time.

Ensrett

TIMELINE

900–1000

Christianity is introduced to Denmark.

1563

A seven-year war between Denmark and Sweden began.

1729

Greenland became part of Denmark.

1914–1918

Denmark was neutral during **World War I**.

1972

Margrethe II was crowned queen.

2012

Helle Thorning-Schmidt became the first female prime minister.

AN IMPORTANT SYMBOL

Denmark's flag is red with a white Scandinavian cross. The Danish flag was adopted in 1625. It is the oldest flag in Europe.

The country is a **constitutional monarchy**. Parliament makes laws. The prime minister is the head of government. The king or queen is the head of state.

In a famous Danish story, Denmark's flag fell from heaven during a 1219 battle. The flag was thought to be a sign from God that Denmark would win.

In June 2015, Lars Løkke Rasmussen became Denmark's prime minister. He was also prime minister from 2009 to 2011.

SAY IT

Lars Løkke Rasmussen
Lahrs Loo-kah RAS-muh-suhn

ACROSS THE LAND

Most of Denmark's land is low. The country has many small lakes and beaches. Denmark is famous for its fjords. These long, narrow pieces of land create deep-sea areas between cliffs. The highest point is called Yding Skovhøj. It stands 568 feet (173 m) high.

Did You Know?

The average winter temperature in Denmark is about 32°F (0°C). Summer temperatures average 63°F (17°C).

The Faroe Islands are about 541 square miles (1,400 sq km) wide. There are 18 major islands.

Much of Denmark's forests were cleared for farmland. However, deer, hares, and hedgehogs still live in the woods. More than 300 kinds of birds live in Denmark. And, the nearby waters are filled with fish such as cod and herring.

Vejlerne is a nature reserve in northern Denmark. It is the largest bird sanctuary in northern Europe.

The gray heron is a common bird in Denmark. They are tall birds with a wingspan of about six feet (2 m). Herons live near bodies of water.

Earning a Living

Animals and farming are important to life in Denmark. Many people fish for a living. Farmers raise cows and pigs. The country's main crops are barley, potatoes, sugar beets, and wheat.

Some Danes are factory workers. They make furniture, machine parts, paper products, processed food, and windmills. Others work in service industries such as banking and health care.

More than 60 percent of Denmark's land is used for farming. Today, about 600,000 dairy cows live in Denmark.

LIFE IN DENMARK

Denmark is known for its arts. The country is home to theaters and ballet companies. Many famous writers are from Denmark.

Danish foods often include meat, especially pork. Denmark's national dish is fried pork with parsley sauce and potatoes. People eat a lot of herring, rye bread, and fried meatballs.

Did You Know?

In Denmark, children must attend school from ages 7 to 16.

The Royal Danish Ballet began in 1771. It is the third-oldest in the world.

Sports are important in Denmark. Soccer continues to be popular. Danish athletes have won Olympic gold medals in events such as cycling and swimming.

In Denmark, people are free to choose their own religion. Most people are **Lutheran**. This faith was established during the 1500s. Today, smaller groups throughout Denmark practice other religions.

The Danish National Soccer Team plays at Parken Stadium in Copenhagen. More than 38,000 people can fit in this stadium.

FAMOUS FACES

Many talented people come from Denmark. Hans Christian Andersen was born in Odense on April 2, 1805. Throughout his life, Andersen worked as an actor and wrote plays. But, he's famous for writing fairy tales.

Today, children around the world know Andersen's fairy tales. His most popular stories include "The Ugly Duckling," "The Princess and the Pea," and "Thumbelina." Andersen died August 4, 1875, in Copenhagen. Many of his fairy tales have become famous movies.

Andersen never married or had children. Instead, he spent much of his time writing.

A statue called *The Little Mermaid* sits on a rock in Copenhagen's harbor. It is based on Andersen's fairy tale.

Caroline Wozniacki was born in Odense on July 11, 1990. She is a tennis player who **competes** all around the world. In 2010, she became the first Danish tennis player to be the world's top-ranked player.

Wozniacki represented Denmark in the 2008, 2012, and 2016 Olympic games. Sadly, she did not win a medal. When she's not playing tennis, Wozniacki creates her own line of tennis clothes.

SAY IT

Caroline Wozniacki
KA-ruh-leyen WAHZ-nee-ack-ee

In 2016, Wozniacki won the Hong Kong Tennis Open.

TOUR BOOK

Imagine traveling to Denmark! Here are some places you could go and things you could do.

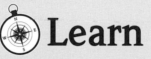 **Learn**

The **Viking** Ship Museum on Roskilde Fjord has five original ships. These boats were built during the 1100s to protect the city.

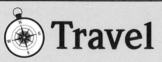 **Travel**

Built in the 1574, the Kronberg Castle is open for tours. The royal family used to live here before the late 1600s.

 Explore

Visit Hans Christian Andersen's home in Odense. The museum opened in 1908. It includes his art, drawings, and writings.

See

During the fall, thousands of birds fill the sky along Denmark's west coast. The birds create dark shapes in the sky.

 Play

Join millions of fans and visit Legoland in Billund. The amusement park has more than 50 rides.

A Great Country

The story of Denmark is important to our world. Denmark is a land with a rich history and famous fairy tales. It is a country of people who want to live in peace.

The people and places that make up Denmark offer something special. They help make the world a more beautiful, interesting place.

The Nyhavn Promenade is a famous waterfront and canal. People visit this area to eat at restaurants along the water.

Denmark Up Close

Official Name: Kingdom of Denmark

Flag:

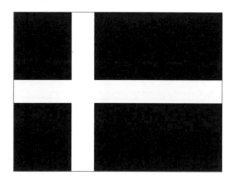

Population (rank): 5,724,456
(July 2016 est.)
(116th most-populated country)

Total Area (rank): 16,639 square miles
(134th largest country)

Capital: Copenhagen

Official Language: Danish

Currency: Danish krone

Form of Government:
Constitutional monarchy

National Anthem: "Der er et yndigt land" ("There Is a Lovely Land") and "Kong Christian" ("King Christian")

IMPORTANT WORDS

capital a city where government leaders meet.

Christianity (krihs-chee-A-nuh-tee) a religion that follows the teachings of Jesus Christ.

compete to take part in a contest between two or more persons or groups.

constitutional monarchy (kahnt-stuh-TOO-shnuhl MAH-nuhr-kee) a form of government in which a king or queen has only those powers given by a country's laws and constitution.

economy the way that a country produces, sells, and buys goods and services.

electronics products that work by controlling the flow of electricity. These often do useful things.

European Union (EU) a group of European countries that works toward political and economic cooperation.

immigration the act of leaving one's home and settling in a new country.

Lutheran a member of a Protestant church who follows the teachings of Martin Luther.

peninsula land that sticks out into water and is connected to a larger piece of land.

Viking one of the Scandinavians who raided or invaded the coasts of Europe from the 700s to 900s.

World War I a war fought in Europe from 1914 to 1918.

World War II a war fought in Europe, Asia, and Africa from 1939 to 1945.

WEBSITES

To learn more about Explore the Countries, visit **abdobooklinks.com**. These links are routinely monitored and updated to provide the most current information available.

INDEX